Layovers

Peggy Pollock

Made with ♥ on the BookLeaf Publishing Platform
www.bookleafpub.in
www.bookleafpub.com

Dedication

to those i have loved for moments in time, and to those who have loved me through them all

Preface

"Art opens the closets, airs out the cellars and attics. It brings healing."
– Julia Cameron

Acknowledgements

i acknowledge you. thanks for being here.

1. Lake Louise

we both like myths and mysteries
we both smoke a little weed
ok, a lot, but that's fine with me
but i don't know if that's enough

we both come from lines of saint and scholars
two scorpio moons who don't like to be bothers
got dreams of leaning in to the farm and the fodder
and that might be enough

we both agree i look cute holding babies
both understand the secret meaning of maybe
comfortable silences, you handle my crazy
and i think it could be enough

we both want to dream in color
accept the invitation, unite and conquer
have our happy hours by the water
but will it always be enough?

cause i like the beach and you like the lake
you drink beer and i like rosé
you say there's room for both if we make room for fate
so that should be enough

i might be a diamond but you like it rough
and i love to be free but i'd hand you the cuffs
so how about we kiss and just shut the fuck up
and let it be enough

2. Alaska

he said i reminded him of alexis rose
a little bit bratty but a heart of gold
a touch of naivety but smarter than you
a former wild thing with a story or two

he said i was trouble and boy was he right
crossing the line just to pass the time
showing off snapshots from his real life
leaning on his shoulder when they dimmed down the
lights

he said are you with him?
i shook my head no, there's nobody waiting for me back
at home
just me and my dog and a big box of wine
that i'd be happy to share if you ever stopped by

he said this is it, i'll see you around?
i'm dropping my stuff and then hitting the town
i said that sounds good, yeah i'll see you later
and he hands me a number written on crumped paper

he said we'll talk later but six hours is all i need
i thought it'd be better to stay a mystery

i never did call him, it's really a shame
cause it's been three years and i still remember his name

but I think it i called him, eventually we'd crash
there'd be too many lovers and not enough cash
the songs so much sweeter when it's frozen in time
and i can always be happy when i think about that flight

3. Paris

do you promise to have and to hold
to aid and abet until we grow old
i've already written the vows in my head
it's you and it's me, in my very best dress

cause i'd play with the others but i'd marry you
i'd look you right in the eyes and tell you "i do"
and my voice wouldn't shake and my hands wouldn't
tremble
i'd promise forever and i'd mean it tenfold

i'll pick the venue, you pick the first dance
you ask the question, i'll say hell yes
and i'll be your darlin', your partner in crime
alls well that ends well as long as you're mine

4. Alcatraz

i still don't know
whose scars are worse
but we're in the thick of winter
so that means springs close

nature always happens
right on time
it's out of my hands
i'm out of my mind

5. Outer Banks

head out to the dunes
with my bag full of journals
one with jokes to make you laugh
one for all my turmoil
one for all my big ideas
one for all my prayers
but it sure would be sweeter
if you could be here

6. Forte

i need someone to hold me
she thought as she cried
well you're not holding yourself
said a voice from the sky
we're all around you
and we're holding you tight
we see all your secrets
the battles you fight
and you might not feel it
but we're holding your hand
and as a matter of fact
we've got a grand plan

for each tear that has fallen
from your big brown sad eyes
plants the seed for a blessing
sure to blow your tiny mind
we've watched how you rise
from the ash like a phoenix
and we've clapped for the moments
you thought nobody witnessed

you're divine and you're brave
but you're never alone

it's just a few more miles
until you make it back home

7. Yankee Stadium

it's all about balance
i say through the smoke
he laughs and he's coughing
hey aren't you broke?

well aren't you broken?
i give it right back
a mutual understanding
of what we both lack

it's all about growing
i say through my tears
he shakes his head slowly
you've said that for years

well this time i mean it
i give it right back
a mutual understanding
of my plan of attack

it's all about boldness
i say through my fear
he looks at his rolex
just finish your beer

well i think that we're done for
i give it right back
a mutual understanding
that i won't be back

8. Bermuda

oh shit here we go again
i got an inch
now i'm playing pretend

i'm pretending you care
pretending it'll stick
you'll send me your playlists
and i'll overanalyze the lyrics

you'll call me angel
you'll write me songs
and just like the rest
once you come you'll be gone

9. Greenwich

13

watching the lightning
from the rooftops in london
three bottles, all empty
didn't care that it's pourin'
a storm was a brewin'
but we wouldn't have known it
cause there was nothing but peace
in those moments you held me

10. Haight-Ashbury

it's your favorite toy
but you don't want to keep it
it's your favorite quote
but you can't seem to speak it
it's the air that you breathe
but you just keep on choking
it's a fork in the road
where the fuck are we going?

11. Minneapolis

we know why the caged bird sings
so why does the free bird cry?
god gave you the feathers
now get up and fly

12. Hillary Step

it's the end of an error
time to rebuild what fell apart
i bought a one way ticket
and still got my rockabilly heart
i let go of all the pain
and found a way to make it art
turns out i've always been the light
even when i was in the dark

13. Loomis Street

here's what you'd do
to even the score
you'd come to my house
you'd knock on my door
you'd ask for my pa
you'd sit on the porch
your voice would be shaking
but you'd have made your choice

you'd say--
can i please have your mentally ill daughter?
i know she don't own much
but i love what you've taught her
how to kill them with kindness
how to be like water
how to bend without breaking
how to fight without fire
and if you give me your blessing
i swear i'll lift her up higher

14. Marlboro

she gave me a warm smile
as she passed by
"that thing takes precious minutes from your precious
life"

i returned her warm smile
as i inhaled again
"a woman's gotta have her vices and it was this or men"

so we left it at that because we both know
those precious minutes of mine, they leave with the
smoke
and death is straight forward, but men give you hope

15. Varosha

i took the outfit saved for our first date
and i painted the whole town red
kind of like the shade of burgundy
you left imprinted on my bed
every moment felt like magic
they're still imprinted in my head
i thought that you would love me
but you destroyed me instead

16. Primrose Hill

i've always lived for the plath of it all
always poured my little heart out
with words on bathroom stalls
and when i saw the fig tree winking
i made sure to follow the call

and i am i am i am

plagued with all of the same doubts
like is everything i write stupid?
like am i talking too loud?
like did i ruin everything?
like will i ever calm down?

and that hallowed jar, oh, it follows me too
even through the streets of paris
even when i'm with you
it's there in every moment
it haunts me like a ghost
no matter how fast i run, it always stays close

and please don't take my picture
when you know i'm going to cry
when i'm trying but i'm failing

to have the time of my life

cause you've got a cripple, a dying man, a whore
then there's me
and the devil is taking bets on who's up first
to be freed

and i don't want flowers
i simply want love
from sailors and soldiers
and our father above

and i'll always be okay
but i'll never be still
i'll write and i'll toil
i'll try to remember my pills

then i'll burn and i'll rise
and i'll claw and i'll scratch
unlike her, i'll survive
unlike her, i will last

cause i don't want to be sylvia
i want to grow old
so long as the moon hangs high
and the sun is gold

17. Philadelphia

i heard you paint houses
she said to the man
sitting in the dark
bourbon in his hand

i heard you paint houses
and i need your help
then she ordered a drink
from the very top shelf

i heard you paint houses
she said after their cheers
and i've had this problem
for so many years

i heard you paint houses
she leaned in real close
and pulled out a blank check
from inside of her coat

i heard you paint houses
their hands intertwined
and i'm begging you sweetly
can you please do mine?

i heard you paint houses
her smile was gone
are you in or not?
we don't have too long

the man sat there in silence
he looked at the girl
put the check in his pocket
asked are you sure

she answered him quickly
there's no doubt about it
come by around 10
when it's usually quiet

thanks for the paint job
he nodded his head
and tomorrow come sunrise
one more will be dead

18. Valinor

you snuck into my room
and you tucked me in
i wore my pjs
you wore a wicked grin
just one quick kiss then off to bed
while a million scenarios run through my head

like me on my knees
your hands in my hair
my sleepy eyes
and your wild stare

you've always held the cards
but i've always run the table
i've got the cheshire grin
and i write the ending to the fable

19. Hudson Valley

time keeps moving
and i've been getting too high
asking myself
have i become the bad guy?

i find the markers that i left
still right there on the trail
wondering how, despite them,
i still failed
i'll escape the woods, even if i'm frail

time keeps moving
but i've been staying right here
haven't eaten
but i'm on my third beer

i check the maps again
but all the signals crossed
i keep reminding myself
not all is lost
the sun is shining, melting through the frost

20. Bald Head Island

every time you ring my line
three hours gone but i don't mind
and i hate talking on the phone
but it's so damn nice to hear your voice

though i never hear what i'm hoping to
like i want you, come see me soon
or don't you spend one more night alone
or babe, i'm finally coming home

and i can't feed you all your lines
can't waste any more of my sweet time
sitting, wishing, waiting on you
singing songs about how love's so cruel

so i'll go on and you'll be mad
wondering why i stopped the dance
and it's pretty simple, you do the math
you had to choose me for this to last

we're going in circles, we've been here before
every god damn night the light beams from my porch
and they say good things come to those who wait
that he'll come back if you give him space

then he'll come in, as a fast as a comet
but time's got me wondering if i even want it

cause, babe, never once did i waver on you
i sent them all packing, broke a heart or two
i'm doing the work and you're doing your thing
not sure if you noticed but i grew some new wings
so i'll keep on flying, though it cuts me to the core
cause i love you honey, but i love me more

too good to be true, that's probably right
you'll have your regrets and i'll be alright

21. Salem

she can try to wear my clothes
she can try to tell my jokes
but that sparkle in her eye ain't gold
she tries, but she ain't me

the wicked surely never rest
but neither do the heaven sent
i'm dodging every spell she sent
those tricks don't work on me

my grace and grit is tried and true
i make the best out of my blues
i'd never want to be like you
i'm quite alright with me

she oughta try to find her shine
stop trying to diminish mine
time to move on, find another guy
cause darlin, you ain't me

you can try but all you'll find is you ain't me